Look There

: : :

BOOKS BY AGI MISHOL

Nanny and Both of Us
Cat Scratch
Gallop
Plantation Notes
Fax Pigeon
The Interior Plain
See (edited by Nathan Zach)
Look There
The Dream Notebook
Wax Flowers
New and Selected Works
Moment

LOOK THERE

New and Selected Poems of

AGI MISHOL

: : :

Translated from the Hebrew by Lisa Katz

Graywolf Press
Saint Paul, Minnesota

Publication of this volume is made possible in part by a grant provided by the Minne-
sota State Arts Board, through an appropriation by the Minnesota State Legislature;
a grant from the Wells Fargo Foundation Minnesota; and a grant from the National
Endowment for the Arts, which believes that a great nation deserves great art. Sig-
nificant support has also been provided by the Bush Foundation; Target and Mervyn's
with support from the Target Foundation; the McKnight Foundation; and other gen-
erous contributions from foundations, corporations, and individuals. To these orga-
nizations and individuals we offer our heartfelt thanks.

MINNESOTA
STATE ARTS BOARD

NATIONAL
ENDOWMENT
FOR THE ARTS

A Lannan Translation Selection
Funding the translation and publication of exceptional literary works

Published by Graywolf Press
2402 University Avenue, Suite 203
Saint Paul, Minnesota 55114
All rights reserved.

www.graywolfpress.org

Published in the United States of America

ISBN 1-55597-436-8

2 4 6 8 9 7 5 3 1
First Graywolf Printing, 2006

Library of Congress Control Number: 2005925174

Cover design: Kyle G. Hunter

Cover art: Menashe Kadishman, *Lamb in Yellow*

Acknowledgments

Some of these translations appeared in earlier versions in the following journals:

The American Poetry Review: excerpts from "Wax Flowers" and
   "Woman Martyr"
The Drunken Boat (thedrunkenboat.com): "A Little Prayer for
   Sunday" and excerpts from *The Dream Notebook*
Leviathan Quarterly: "The Peacock," "[I stand in an open field],"
   "Eros Pedagogitis," and "Olive Tree"
Mississippi Review online (mississippireview.com): "To the Muses"
   and "Monday"
PIW: Poetry International Web (Rotterdam) (poetryinternational
   .org): "Woman Martyr," "A Little Prayer for Sunday," and
   "Transistor Muezzin"
Poetry International (San Diego State, California): "Papua, New
   Guinea" and "Swimmers"
Prairie Schooner: "Horse" and "Monday"
Runes: "White Chicken"
Tikkun: "Olive Tree"
A View from the Loft: "November 4, 1995"
World Literature Today: "Woman Martyr" and "To the Muses"

Translator's Acknowledgments: I want first of all to thank Agi Mishol for patiently unraveling with me the puzzles in her words, "wrinkled within . . . like the silk of a flower inside a bud." I want to return love to the doubly hyphenated American-Israeli poet-translators Shirley Kaufman and Rachel Back, who read the translations in many incarnations, offering warmth and welcome suggestions, and to offer affectionate thanks to Natasha Sajé, poet and professor, who willingly served as my ideal American reader from her home in Salt Lake City, and during a Fulbright stay in Ljubljana. I want to thank Dr. Eynel Wardi, of the Hebrew University English Department, who slipped "The Peacock" to me and started this book on its way, unbeknownst to both of us, and warmly acknowledge editors Jeff Shotts and Anne Czarniecki, who completed the transition from manuscript to physical book with professional ease. I want to offer my heartfelt thanks to the *Poetry International Web* project, based in Rotterdam, of which I am lucky to be a part, and especially to Corine Vloet, who suggested I write for *PIW* about translating Mishol, and to the Israeli national editor Rami Saari, poet and translator par excellence, my role model. I want to thank my Literary Translation students at Hebrew University and Ben Gurion University, from whom I learn what sensitive readers of Hebrew feel. Most of all, I ask my children Carmi and Maya to consider this effort my gift to them, a paean to their languages. And it nearly went without saying that neither they nor this book would exist without S. L., who brought us into being here.

—LK

Contents

from *The Dream Notebook* (2000)

from *Look There* and Earlier Poems (1972–1999)

Introduction: "God in the Details"

> In contemporary Israeli poetry, intense, white flames
> appear against the dark, burning background. . . . Those
> with eyes in their heads can see: Agi Mishol's poetry is
> one of the brightest of these flames.
>
> : *Dan Miron, Leonard Kaye*
> *Professor of Hebrew Literature,*
> *Columbia University*

Have you ever splashed past an older person in a swimming lane and felt a flash of superiority accompanied by a twinge of fear? Agi Mishol seized this wisp of consciousness before it evaporated in the overheated air of the pool. She fashioned it into a poem in which smugness masks a denial of death, now couched in the language of swimming:

> And we haven't got any pity for these pretenders.
> On the contrary:
> with broad hints we turn them out
> to their rightful place, which certainly isn't among us,
> the swimmers
> who don't care to keep abreast just now
> of the goal we dive toward.

Agi Mishol is a master of detail, which makes her work eminently translatable, despite the many linguistic and cultural differences between the Hebrew and English languages, because details have a way of being serendipitous in every language. She records, often with rueful amusement, the minutiae of ordinary life in a tiny Mediterranean country, including its flora and fauna—with which she, as a farmer,

is well acquainted—and the sharply-observed, smallest details of her
nightly dreams, a love affair, the appreciation of a little happiness—
from modest pleasures—on a Monday:

> The chicory flowers'
> morning blue,
> the entire meadow,
> a cluster of snails
> on top of a sea onion stalk,
> and there was also the word "wagtail."
> What else was there?

Released in 2003, Mishol's *New and Selected Works*—her famil-
iar face and trademark blond curls stenciled in bright colors on the
cover—moved into a fifth printing within a year. It has already been
followed by a new volume, *Moment*, whose title recalls the amorous
experiences recounted within and a Jerusalem café destroyed by a
suicide bomber. Six of these poems appear in the opening section of
this book, Mishol's first full-length work to appear in English.

In her work, Agi Mishol doesn't merely "look there," stroking our
egos for recognizing the familiar. She commits subversive acts of es-
trangement. For example, it may take readers a little while to realize
that in the heaven imagined in her *The Dream Notebook*, no human
beings will materialize on the list of blessed inhabitants. Instead,
heaven includes dogs, well-groomed or abandoned, and less attrac-
tive creatures that most of us seek to eliminate as pests, and that's it:

> the poodle from the Humane Society was there
> and the mongrel from the road to Rehovot
> and the one abandoned in the Yavneh station
> and not only:

generations of cats whose spirits were refreshed
by the Friskies kit I keep in my car,
puppies from the coastal plain,
one frozen heron I fan-dried in winter,

mice I returned to the field from the house,
spiders I saved from the cleaning lady's broom,
a porcupine whose fleas I removed
with a tweezer
all of them
all of them were there

Mishol has not flinched from aiming her defamiliarizing glance at her immediate environment, Israel in the twenty-first century. One aspect of the Israeli-Palestinian conflict over land is the uprooting of trees. Olive trees provide a living to many Palestinian farmers, but have suffered uprooting in areas bordering on Israeli settlements, especially over the last five years, ostensibly in order to clear the sides of the roads in the occupied areas and prevent attacks on Israelis who live in them. Mishol's poem does not convey an extreme ecological view that trees are more important than people. It is rather that Mishol is able to record her ethical dilemma about the conflict between people inside the detail about vegetation. Some of these trees, it is imagined in the poem, and it may be so in life, turn up for sale at plant nurseries in shopping malls in the new, suburban Israel, (its sprawl made possible by the encroachment on Palestinian land). The trees are now important only as garden decoration, and so the unpicked olives "blacken," as does the speaker's face—for abetting the waste of nature and human effort which is caused by the political situation:

Olive Tree

shafted, stuck among three coconut palms
in the red earth of a tub from the Home Depot
in the middle of a junction turned overnight
into a square.

Motorists hurrying home
see it perhaps
through clay pots tilting over,
but they have no time for the twisted story
that rises from its trunk or the flat top of the tree,
trimmed with a building contractor's sense of humor.

Nor can they fathom their roots groping
in foreign soil
clutching mother earth
like provisions from home
since the soldiers cut them down.

The olives, offered and unwanted, blacken
my face
and no miniature roses will divert my heart
from the shame.

We had a disagreement during the translation of this poem: the original Hebrew manages to convey a fact (that soldiers cut down olive trees) in one word—military newspeak, the euphemistic neologism *khee-soof*, a noun created from the Hebrew root which means "to bare," or "to clear away." The original sentence ends, literally, succinctly, with "the uproar of the clearing" and no further words are needed for people who read Israeli newspapers in Hebrew daily. Mishol objected to my explanatory translation "the soldiers cut them down" and preferred to use the apparently equivalent word "clear-ing," without mentioning the soldiers. In the end, we compromised on "military uproar." But then I insisted on restoring the soldiers, for I found "military uproar" to be an impenetrable concept, and the word "uproar" implicit in the action of the soldiers. I recount this in-cident because it embodies a classic process that occurs when trans-lating. A word in the original does so much work, linguistically and culturally, that it seems to the translator that only an explanatory phrase will make sense in translation. To the writer, who intuitively carried the word into an ironic new context in her poem, and to a bi-lingual reader of source and target languages, the substitution seems excessive, unacceptable.

Given the situation in Israel and in nascent Palestine, there is no lack of political detail for Mishol to examine closely. After a woman terrorist detonates herself in the public market in Jerusalem, Mishol feels unable to avoid repeating the sensational "story, / about which I speak all the time / without having anything to say." Mishol's "Woman Martyr" contains no summary statements, and offers no moral to the story; significance, if it can be claimed at all, emerges from the details observed. Mishol has said that she was moved to write the poem, as others, because of a marginal element: the woman suicide bomber's surname — Takatka — sounds like the Hebrew word for ticking, *(leh-tak-tek)*. That the woman is named may be consid-ered a humanizing element, and some Israeli readers of the original Hebrew poem seemed to think that Mishol approved of women mar-tyrs and suicide bombers: angry letters were written to the newspaper in which the poem first appeared, and subscriptions were cancelled. However, in humanizing the inhuman, the poem is not expressing approval of Takatka's act, but rather evincing, as Israeli poet Rami Saari says, a very "human intention to make the unbearable at least understandable and so to reduce the amount of horror."

A linguistic blank in this poem for readers of the translation may be the fact that the Hebrew name of the town of Bethlehem consists of two words—*beit lekhem*—literally meaning "house (or home) of bread." The poem in Hebrew ironically notes that Takatka, even though she came from Bethlehem, the home of bread, chose to detonate herself in a bakery—while she herself seems to embody bread rising, swelling with pregnancy. Furthermore, the word "bread" in Hebrew *(lekhem)* means "meat" in Arabic *(lakhm)*, as well as possibly having some relation to the Hebrew word for fighting and war *(lekh-ee-ma)*, which it recalls; in this way the Hebrew language evokes linguistic and other differences between the warring peoples, and one source of difference—fighting over the land that provides people with a living, and puts food on the table, bread and meat. In this instance, the translation into English brings about a surprising and significant change in the poem, because English is likely to evoke the New Testament, a text that is not part of Israeli Jewish culture. In English, Bethlehem is associated with the birth of Christ, and the bread also connotes Christ himself as the metaphorical "bread of life."

Unforeseen and quirky shifts may occur in all translation. Changes in translating from Hebrew (sometimes compensated for by the addition of explanatory phrases, and sometimes not) exist, paradoxically, because of the special opportunity that Hebrew offers to its poetry: a limited number of two- or three-letter roots, from which words are developed. Mishol says with delight: "If I think 'womb' *(reh-khem)* and 'compassion' *(rakh-ah-meem)*—show me another language that has a semantic connection between the two." Mishol also mentions a group of words (developed from a different root) that includes "north" *(tsa-phone)*, "hidden" *(tsa-phoon)*, "conscience" *(mats-poon)*, and "compass" *(mats-pen)*. "Where indeed is our [moral] sense of direction?" she asks. "Hidden, encoded deep within us, within our consciences, and hard to locate." So the letters in Hebrew words seem, magically, to connect ideas that are not evoked by equivalent English words. One only needs to think of the way Greek-influenced languages connect "womb" *(hustera)* to hysteria to realize how arbitrary these connections actually are.

And then there is the issue of intertextuality. How might readers in English know what Mishol has read in her own culture, unless they were also students of that culture? In the case of the bomber poem, paratextual information in an epigraph seems to me to work very well in translation. Mishol quotes a poem by Israeli writer Nathan Alterman (1910–1970), "Late Afternoon in the Market," which addresses a woman, presumably a Jewish one, passing by in the marketplace: "The evening goes blind, / and you are only twenty." The forces of nature seem to have the upper hand in Alterman's poem: first the evening "goes blind"—the sun goes down with a momentary blinding flash as it moves below the horizon, and the earth is darkened, blinded as it were—and only then is the young woman an object of consideration. In Israel today, in Mishol's poem, the order is reversed: a young woman can darken the day. Or perhaps, the situation is actually the same: the blinding of day is not caused by nature but rather by a young woman—in the first poem by her beauty and in the second by her bomb.

The direct address to and concern for and about the blindingly beautiful woman in Alterman's poem cannot help but be turned toward Mishol's terrorist, who is directly addressed in the first line of her poem with exactly the same words, whether one reads in Hebrew or in English or any other language. In the rich and strange way that poetry makes meaning, Alterman's anonymous young woman as a traditionally romanticized (if feared) object *overlaps* with Mishol's bomber as a terrifying and failed woman (experiencing a murderous, fake pregnancy).

Born in 1947 in Hungary, Mishol arrived in Israel as a very young child, speaking Hungarian at home and Hebrew outside. "My mother's tongue is not my mother tongue," she often says. She earned her BA and MA in Hebrew literature from the Hebrew University, her first volume of poetry appearing in 1972. She lives on a peach and persimmon farm, and teaches creative writing workshops at the major universities, and literature at Alma College in Tel Aviv. She is a frequent lecturer at literary venues, and at some that are not: she recently lectured about poetry to hundreds of members of the science faculty at Israel's Technion University (roughly equivalent to MIT), and about language to the Lawyer's Guild at its annual convention. She has been awarded every major Israeli poetry prize, and is regularly invited to international festivals; in 2004, she was the first Israeli poet to appear at the Berlin Poetry Festival, where she read with the Palestinian poet Mahmoud Darwish. In Israel, a group of her poems have been dramatized in a play, *The Owl Ladies*, and a jazz CD based on *Moment* is about to be released.

The only child of Holocaust survivors—the sequence *Wax Flowers* is dedicated to them—Mishol does not write "Holocaust poems" per se. Rather, its memory hovers near her poems the way it hovers over Israeli culture, emerging in displaced details, fading only to return: "rusting" in the eyes of a dying survivor, and reprised in the eyes of cattle bound for slaughter on a truck, seen by chance at a stoplight.

During some of the most murderous moments of the current stage of fighting between Israel and the Palestinians, I interviewed Mishol in her home in a rural area of Gedera, a town near the coast. A modest rectangular house protected by shrubs from the road and with orchards behind it, with three lazy-looking, mixed-breed dogs sunning themselves on the patio, Mishol's home reminds one more of Iowa than Israel.

Against this pastoral environment, she spoke about the sources of poetry. About "To the Muses" she said: "I was standing over here in the yard, yellow flowers were in bloom over there, it was just beautiful. Naturally this is how one wants things to be, to write about the subjects poetry is drawn to—beauty, eternity, which don't exist *for* anything, poetry doesn't exist *for* anything, it doesn't have a goal, it's not about statements. Beauty isn't *for* something. And poetry as I experience it is usually born out of quietness, nothingness. That's poetry's natural background. I often think about it as the image of a fish in water: living in it, the fish doesn't notice the water. Poetry too lives inside this nothingness. Inside the quiet. It develops slowly. And suddenly the background changes and it's noisy because of the changes and so poetry changes too—it can't be what it generally is."

"And so poetry changes too." Agi Mishol's work exemplifies poetry that emerges from a particular and particularly talented individual at a particular moment in history, and responds to a particular natural environment and political situation, and which manages to become universal without being general. In "The Comic Sybil," Dan Miron's afterword to her *New and Selected Works*, the noted scholar and critic makes a case for Mishol as a shaper of culture:

> Agi Mishol's poetry acts not only in the literary-poetic field of an Israeli culture struggling to consolidate itself; it also makes a broader attempt to shape a way of life and a world view. For her part Mishol contributes to this effort the splendid example of the possibility of moving from imbalance to equilibrium; from diving down in the depths of the self to knowledge of the world and consideration for the Other; from an enthusiastic affinity for the pleasure principle to the ability to combine it with a more courageous connection to reality, without losing grasp of joy. It is difficult to exaggerate the importance of this balanced cultural model in the midst of a cultural reality which has no mental and intellectual equilibrium whatsoever.

You will be the judge about whether these poems live in English, but it seems to me that when we read poetry, meaning unfolds in associative figural chains that begin with words and phrases. Because any poem's chains of associations are culture-linked, original and translation must be different, the way poems allow for different readings even in the source language; poem and translation are alike only in the rather abstract "universal" way that cultures are alike, if they are alike. Perhaps the relationship between original and translation, so difficult to articulate, is encompassed by Walter Benjamin's enigmatic statement that "the task of the translator [is] to release in his own language that pure language which is under the spell of another."

The "pure language" might be something like sex experienced in our minds, which we also sometimes live with our bodies, with the bodies of others, in very particular ways. As Agi Mishol writes in "Moment":

> I could have trembled with you under the covers
> but I can also make you tremble inside my head
> inside the thick stuff of alchemy
> from which poems are made.

Lisa Katz
Jerusalem
June 2005

:::

from *Moment* and Other New Poems

(2003–2005)

Moment

: : :

In the beginning were the words.
After that I heard the boom.

: : :

How can I reach your heart,
you, with a womb in your brain.

: : :

Cupids leap from your brow,
armed with tear gas,
that's for sure.

: : :

Signs:
my amethyst necklace
rhymes with your purple
silk
shirt.

: : :

You're not in my pocket
but rustle there
like the wrapper of a candy
saved for later.

:::

I've already learned to stroke myself
with inner breaths of air,
but my fakery is such that if someone
merely touches me softly
all the weeping spills outside,
rolling like a river
to the sea.

:::

To fondle,
that's what I want,
to cling to you
moving slowly,
I'm
all senses.

:::

I want you to play me
with your fingers
that suddenly spiral
to the sides
like a bird waking up,
(when you demonstrate
how Nietzsche thought)
separating quills from feathers
so beautifully.

:::

(Perhaps I'll stun you.
Like a robber I'll drag you
into my cave.)

:::

You stroke me with your wisdom.
I feel it,
like an overcompensated sense of touch
developed at the expense
of some darkness,
of a different kind.

:::

I could have trembled with you under the covers
but I can also make you tremble inside my head
inside the thick stuff of alchemy
from which poems are made.

Woman Martyr

The evening goes blind, and you are only twenty.
: Nathan Alterman,
"Late Afternoon in the Market"

You are only twenty
and your first pregnancy is a bomb.
Under your broad skirt you are pregnant with dynamite
and metal shavings. This is how you walk in the market,
ticking among the people, you, Andaleeb Takatka.

Someone loosened the screws in your head
and launched you toward the city;
even though you come from Bethlehem,
the Home of Bread, you chose a bakery.
And there you pulled the trigger out of yourself,
and together with the Sabbath loaves,
sesame and poppy seed,
you flung yourself into the sky.

Together with Rebecca Fink you flew up
with Yelena Konre'ev from the Caucasus
and Nissim Cohen from Afghanistan
and Suhila Houshy from Iran
and two Chinese you swept along
to death.

Since then, other matters
have obscured your story,
about which I speak all the time
without having anything to say.

Olive Tree

shafted, stuck among three coconut palms
in a layer of gravel from the Home Depot
in the middle of a junction turned overnight
into a square.

Motorists hurrying home
see it perhaps
through clay pots tilting over,
but they have no time for the twisted story
that rises from its trunk or the flat top of the tree,
trimmed with a building contractor's sense of humor.

Nor can they fathom their roots groping
in foreign soil
clutching mother earth
like provisions from home
since the soldiers cut them down.

The olives, offered and unwanted, blacken
my face
and no miniature roses will divert my heart
from the shame.

Red Hail

What's the rush?
Why are you clutching the gearshift?
Why are you hoarding mineral water?

What's this longing
for the wings of a dove
to fly away to the wilderness?

In this muscular and mustached time
find yourself a hiding place
in the Holy Tongue

squeeze yourself into the bookshelves
crouch in the crannies of punctuation marks

live within prepositions
enter the belly of the letter "B"
so your language won't get confused

curl up like a snail inside the letter "S"
inside a "P"
force yourself into the periods

and from the shelter of the letter "D"
send the periscope of an "L" to check
whether the missiles are receding.

Nothing bad will happen to you
if you stick to the lines.
Absorbed in the letters
thou shall not want.

To the Muses

Forgive me, O eternal ones,
for disturbing you with our history
repeating itself

exactly the way the smart wildflowers return,
and the purple loosestrife spreads over my lawn,
but suddenly it's hard to be gratified by beauty
whose entire aim is itself.

Heavenly ones, floating among gauze scarves,
ivory combs in your golden hair,
what do you have in common with the old women in the
    Kandahar hills
gathering crab grass to feed the swollen-bellied children,
or the women bending over the rubble in Rafah
like poisonous black mushrooms rising from the ruins.

How well I know the language of your wildflowers.
I won't trouble you to sneak away with me
in the middle of the night
to pet laboratory monkeys,
or plant compassion in the heart of the farmer
burning the horns off a calf's skull.

But don't turn my eyes today
toward the pink edge of the cloud castle,
don't signal the triumph of eternity
in the birds' V.

To a Young Poet About to Read Aloud

The fairy still grazes the edge of your soul
and lavishes you with beginners' gifts.
You sense her inside the letters
gathering in your testicles,
in the semi-darkness igniting
and swarming in your pupils,
in the way your heart hops like a little bird
under your T-shirt:
fear not

the path is still wrinkled within you
like the silk of a flower inside a bud,
the thickening you cough aside
to clear a trail to your voice
is only noise concealing silence,
just an internal ink hemorrhage,
a thicket of expressions
masking the face you put on
when your turn arrives.

From the audience, limp as water,
I accompany you, watching
the present moment
become a memory, a pinch
from tomorrow's past:
fear not

even though the nights may lengthen
and the angels grow stricter —
the no-exit angels,
the two-faced angel,
the angel of whoring hearts
and the angels of flattery —

you will be consoled by lovers into whose hair,
maddened and short of breath, you murmur unbelievable
    soundtracks,
lovers who stick to the lining of your soul
like scale to the sides of the coffee pot
from which you will drink with the ministering angel
in wordless times.

And you will be consoled by your life's
necessary witness,
the one who listens to your poems
in the electrified pacing up and down the streets
until dawn.

The fairy still grazes your soul,
riffling your pages.
Soon you will stand,
and into the microphone,
as into a big ear,
you will whisper,
for the first time,
your secret.

Scheherazade

It's me, the Scheherazade of poems.
I don't know how much time I have left
between between breath and death.

The gods have given me an unusual punishment.
The more I'm exposed, the more I'm consumed.
When we touch each others' faces,
my immortality dwindles in your heart.

Sultan of talk,
look how I get tangled in the veils.

I don't want to freeze untouched on a pedestal
in the balcony of your harem.
With all this silent worship,
even if I glow like the morning star
what good will it do?

Stop the mouse that scurries through your fingers.
Stop playing the noiseless keyboard.
What good are brains without love,
eyes without the right click?

Hang up the swarm of your head,
and rest in me,
longing (don't worry) never ends
and the soul, like a firefly
flickers, flickers.

My best poems are written when I'm alone
licking the wounds of tiny arrows.
When I die in your heart that thirsts for thirst,
you will be immortal
when you awake.

Eros Pedagogitis

First I'll lick the heart
of your upper lip
slowly, as if applying lipstick:
to the right
to the left
from the point
where the wings spread
upward

and then down the slopes of irony
along the line that restrains
your childish laughter,
and drains toward the corners,
trembling like rabbit noses
at so many contradictions.

Afterward I'll let you speak
your Midas words
into the microphone
on the stage.

You'll talk
and I'll just watch,
flinging tiny lassoes
toward your lower lip
until the jewelry in my brain
chimes through my body
and I press my mouth
against your oxymoron lips.

Pigeons

Pigeons are a pain in the ass.
He was never one of those pigeon lovers
scattering seed from brown paper bags. In fact,
he really can't stand them — pigeons, not turtledoves —
how they fan out over the squares, thrust themselves
into homes, niches, cornices, ledges,
people have no idea how the white droppings corrode everything:
shrubs, sidewalks, not to mention statues,
where they perch profanely on the heads of commanders
spoiling the swing toward eternity,
streaming bird droppings and hurling humor
at the most unexpected places, at poetry too —
he thinks pigeons grossly overrated when they multiply
in the context of innocence, flood and peace. He, for example,
has never seen a dove with an olive branch,
or a poem about the tiny lice that fill the house
and you scratch like a madman after despairing
of the special foil or the slick stuff you buy at the hardware store
and smear on the windowsills. Just look how they
stick out their necks and regret them back into place again,
among all the flapping clucking and feather plucking,
even someone with a talent for the sublime sees
how they shit freely on everything and yet how certain women
decorate their lapels with doves.
Fish are another story
entirely.

Summer in the City

Doves of peace shit a bit and fly off,
the sun a bull's-eye
overhead
and yet people still
stroke each other's skin, apply
word bandages, move from home to heart
or into other people,
because the eyes around us are gunfire sockets,
the reptilian brain already shooting,
and yet in the middle of all this,
people still give massages,
smear oil, roll joints
for other people
crowded into second-rate groups
to bake wafers for the moon, to listen to
what's up,
more and more people move
from home to heart or into other people,
excellent in emergencies,
they manage to pass through the darkness under the covers
reading the Braille of each other's skin with their fingertips
whispering my wife my husband my beloved
and if you should ask me how I'm doing,
you'll feel as though you just shot a bird.

Monday

So what did we have?
The sweet scent of jasmine,
the painted orange sun
discovered suddenly
while cutting the persimmon in half
at the first volley of light.
The chicory flowers'
morning blue,
the entire meadow,
a cluster of snails
on top of a sea onion stalk
and there was also the word "wagtail."
What else was there?
The cicada requiem,
pink sheep in the sloping sky,
and the soft, much-kissed down
on the bottom of the cat's ear
and that's it, I think
that's what we had
today.

:::

from *Wax Flowers*

(2002)

Wax Flowers

:::

I don't know you
to tell the truth
you don't know me either.

I see barbed wire rusting in your eyes
in the evening when your soul hollows
opposite the television console,
in your arms a small tuna salad
together with dry toast

but your mother tongue is not my mother tongue
so we prefer to take a walk:
walking is better than sitting,
sitting is better than lying down,
lying down is better than sleeping

and we walk,
your arm linked in mine,
and we play
"once upon a time"
that I was your mother
and now you are mine.

: : :

At Kastina junction
you peer at me suddenly
from the eyes of the cows
packed into the slaughterhouse truck.

In my fright I memorize
the numbers branded on their backs

the red light in the traffic signal seethes

my eyes stay on the yellow one
which will sort us to the right or left
to life or death.

:::

The gynecologist who examined your womb
wrote in your file:
Total Prolapse,
and I translated: the destruction of the First Temple.

:::

Beyond the doorframe,
also trapped in neon time,
an old lady without underpants
talks to God.

Actually she's addressing a pigeon
wedged into the concrete niche
of the hospital window.

Perhaps the white bird
will take pity on her neighbor,
drained of her strength
and fluttering now
behind the nylon curtain,
between the electric cymbals
conducted by the doctor on duty.

:::

At night in my bed
I fulfill your wish
to lie on your side with your knees bent.
Afterward in a dream I sink into
your brown angora sweater
soft as love
simple as a peanut.

:::

Every morning I bring you
pretty little homemade sandwiches
so you'll have
beautiful words of bread
to pacify Mister Death:
oatmeal,
sprouts,
I bring you pumpernickel, seven grain
bread
if you'd only eat,

eat health bread against death
whole wheat against emptiness.

:::

I didn't have to turn you into the ambulance. If only
I could have smuggled you
to my veterinarian
to put you to sleep
away from here

I would have cradled
your head and whispered *good girl good girl*
until the contractions of death ended
as long as it took
until you birthed yourself
into the other side.

: : :

From day to day
the robin redbreasts
on your robe
are fading

but wherever I go
I return to you
like the mobile phone
to the charger.

:::

Someone lit the wax flowers in your garden,
it's unbelievable how they've blossomed for you,
the whole garden—
you should have seen for yourself—

: : :

About that new baby crow.
I've been chewing pecans for him
for a month already.
I should have told you.

I didn't tell you how he lay against my heart
and loved when I whistled "Aranjuez."

I'm writing him down here
even if he's just a subplot in our story
and his death along with yours,
to my way of thinking,
is an unnecessary exaggeration
by the omniscient narrator.

The bird's presence
would have been enough.

Every raven after Poe
is Nevermore.

: : :

In the death announcements
they stuck you near some engineer.
Even now, after he's shed
this world,
he still wears a ghostly title
while you, finally,
lie next to an engineer.

: : :

The ceremony was modest.
A government clerk handed me
your final papers. You
who never graduated anything
were suddenly entitled to a lovely
death certificate
with the symbol of the state
as if you had mastered something
and fulfilled all the requirements.

She asked me if I wanted to update
(that's what she said)
father's death certificate.
Then she placed them side by side
like a pair of matching gravestones
and pressed the electric buzzer.

I went down to the street
walking
like a little girl
holding the hands
of paper parents
flapping in the wind.

Gravity, Death

How resistance to the force of gravity has weakened:
hair falls out, jaws drop, and legs don't step
off the earth anymore.
The spent body stoops over the ground,
only a walking stick separates them like a kind of extension.

He sits opposite me in a cloud of unraveling sentences,
his skin like clothing hastily left behind
on a chair.

For a moment I sit with my father, for a moment with my death
fraternizing with me through my crumbling father who begins
to return spirit unto spirit
and dust unto dust.

:::

When I died I was already
completely numb

from everything that was there
I remember
a terrible thirst for air

and the silly smile
of my teeth
resting without me
in a cup.

[Told to me by my father the night after he died]

Reconciliation

My father, old and tired,
returned from the dead
to nap on the armchair in my living room.

He arrived in his good clothes—
suit and tie,
a European who happened upon Asiatics.

I am my parents' parent now
and bear no grudge.
I sneak up
to give him
a manly slap
on the back:

"What a nerd you are, Dad,"
I tell him
meaning the type of man
I am doomed to fall in love with all my life.

Parting

As punishment for dying
they exile you now
to a new town
with very small houses.

Wrapped in white
traveling clothes —
that ancient style,
you are stripped
of your first name

and against your will —
block, section, row,
they give you a different address.

I scratch my fingers
on the thorns of blue-moon roses
in my arms,
their fresh scent wafting upward

and watch how they plant you
in the great field of the dead
where no rain
even the most flattering
will cause you to grow, ever again,
in the world.

:::

from *The Dream Notebook*

(2000)

The Dream Notebook

There is a difference between dream poems and poems about dreams. Dream poems are extracted and saved from awareness in time, before the involvement of the brain, whose nature is to think. They preserve the dream atmosphere and its logic of otherness.

:::

(Just before
for a thousandth of a second
I knew for certain
the secret of life
even if my winnings rose up against me
and I forgot as soon as I remembered
and nothing remained
except the sense of knowing)

: : :

If I open my eyes now
my soul will spill blue
over pink

and if I don't open them
the tango will drag me away
to Hernando's Hideaway
in three beats

:::

When I swam in my brain, that cosmic soup
I met another dreamer
who happened into my dream, saying:
if you want to get there,
swim butterfly

:::

I'm being filmed. In the clip
I stride into the ocean
on the heels of my lover who has sailed
far away.

When my red dress balloons over the water,
like a bell in which I'm the clapper,
I'll dive into the depths
and they'll project onto me:
      Fin

:::

I, Marilyn, circulate among the other dreamed figures at a cocktail party, beautiful people. I'm wearing a black evening gown with broad straps that cross in the back designed to hide the stumps of my wings. In one hand, a glass of champagne, a smoking cigarette holder in the other, my butterfly eyes slant every which way as I gaily dispense smiles and small talk.

Only I know about the dress strap business or that's what I think until an usher enters the room, points at me and announces sardonically: "The lady of the chickens." Everyone is stunned into silence when the man approaches and in one swoop removes my dress with a gloat; pearl-spotted chickens began to cluck and scatter filling the room with feathers and flight while something inside me, as if disbelieving, mutters again and again: "What a pain!"

:::

I was alone but in plural watching four poisonous green apples eddying down the sink; just one glance was enough to arouse loud malicious laughter from the depths of the drain and draw the apples down into its underworld.

The balance was off and it was impossible to increase the volume of my cries for help when apple chunks began shooting out like pits; nevertheless two primeval husbands answered me from somewhere, pulling a woman golem out of the garbage disposal and saving her, bringing silence down on the dream.

From there on things moved swiftly and efficiently: the pinkish woman was whisked into the backyard and tied to the lower grindstone, and at the end of three spins (her face to the ground) she hopped and turned into a happy little lamb in the arms of the taller husband.

:::

Identical pairs of Charlie Chaplins and ginger cats the size of people, like husbands and their wives, sit facing me in the very first row. Out of stage fright and perhaps because the lights are dimming, I can't tell at first that the orchestra and even the balconies are filled with them, sitting quietly, exact duplicates, one pair next to another, eyes glued to the film projected onto me. That was the moment I understood that I was the screen, and the only way to discover who I was would be to guess what was being projected, to decipher the miniscule twitches of their mustaches.

:::

Under a lemon tree in my backyard sits José Ortega y Gasset. He wears an army uniform (reserves, apparently) and his job is to put my feelings into words in a literary way. Lemons suit the man with three names, his unfriendly, aristocratic features keeping a proper distance from reality.

I feel and listen, listen and feel, ready out of gratefulness to bend my life towards the wonderfully refined phrases emerging from the quiet toward which they point.

:::

A very tall and worried Japanese woman kneels before me (her head reaches my chest). I have no idea who I am but she knows, otherwise she wouldn't be here with me, upset about something, her eyes slanting in awe, pleading with me not to leave the realm, not now.

She approaches with a rare gesture that says she knows she's exceeding her bounds this once, begins to stroke my back, her last chance at persuasion: she, my chief lady-in-waiting, porcelain-featured, loves me more than is allowed, if that is possible, can't live without me in the palace.

I take in her words. As she empties of speech I fill with self-knowledge, but her stroking distracts me from the thick imperial stuff coursing through my veins and I must make a decision fast:

whether to continue to listen to talk of the palace revolution I've apparently decided to flee, or give up on my curiosity to know who I am and melt into her strokes maddening my senses.

:::

I woke up on the wrong side of the bed.
I haven't been properly developed,
I was supposed to be shiny
and I turned out matte.

: : :

I push my new husband Stephen Hawking in his wheelchair over Swiss mountain ridges, balancing what emerges from his right lobe and disappears diagonally leftward, I shoot a glance at the forested landscape, happy to discover a rope ladder hanging down from a pine tree because stretching is terrific for his disease. The place is also perfect for writing memoirs in old age and the cuckoo bursting from my brain accuses me of marrying him just for this.

:::

As I ascended to heaven
and opened the gate uncertainly,
no magi shone within
just a huge white furry Great Pyrenees
sprawling on a cushion in the place of honor,
and around him, all the animals, down to the last detail:

the poodle from the Humane Society was there
and the mongrel from the road to Rehovot
and the one abandoned in the Yavneh station
and not only these:

generations of cats whose spirits were refreshed
by the Friskies kit I keep in my car,
puppies from the coastal plain,
one frozen heron I fan-dried in winter,

mice I returned to the field from the house,
spiders I saved from the cleaning lady's broom,
a porcupine whose fleas I removed
with a tweezer
all of them
all of them were there

the Great Pyrenees' tenderness
and the mercy in his eyes
filled the animals and the temple

not one word remained in the world
all of them
passed away
passed away

and only my love quoted his love,
my head resting forever on his fur.

: : :

I stand in an open field, biplanes fly maneuvers overhead. A cosmic newscaster announces with cheerful pathos: "The war is over, and, as usual, let's swing the sea-cow in the air."

Amid the silence descending in the sky, a cow appears slowly east of the dream, with black and yellow spots, looking silly; a huge plastic cow sails through the sky, propelled by her limbs as though swimming in the air, and about to announce a blessed peace settling on the world.

I don't make the smallest move, let the peace fall on my head, an audience of one to this fateful event. And then, to the clash of cymbals, as in a magic trick, the cow vanishes, and in its place two identical women shine, Siamese fairies reconciling in the new era of peace, but neither one of us knows which Agi she is.

:::

from *Look There* and Earlier Poems
(1986–1999)

Poem for the Imperfect Man

with all his flaws, loved and indulged,
just as he is—a self divided and angry
hungry thirsty grumbling and hovering
over the void—
a poem for the man ejected without a caress
from night dreams to day dreams
coughing and groping for his shoes
just as he is, intestines crowing
pushing something that will soon be
feces, and meditating on the hunger for love
the horrid horrid hunger for love
many coffees will not quench
this is a poem for the lazy stream of his thoughts,
for the man just as he is, vague and confused,
plucked upward, longing for something,
a poem for a wound
that is not hemorrhaging,
for the knot of silent indignity,
for the cigarette supporting him
as he settles in at his desk
as if sitting down to silence at last.
This is a poem for his pristine pages, a kiss
for his eyes finding rest in the feathery clouds.

A *Little Prayer for Sunday*

Give me a break
from flashing cops,
from HMOs and the temples
of social security,
from talking with my accountant,
and the Manpower jargon
of clerks
with helmet-like hair.

The partridge hunters
have been shooting here all morning,
and the dogcatcher
roams my village.
Newspapers—
filled with black-fisted Orthodox men,
and high-strung poetry critics,
and openmouthed bulldozers—
fall like leaves upon my house.

Why is it such a big deal to yield
to a woman like me
who lets other drivers
cut her off?

I who go to sleep with the hens
at the foot of the well-lit shopping malls—
Hear my prayer—

Please don't lay me down in the culture basket.

I who am not exempt from anything—
grant me
one day off
from the army.

The Swimmers

Old ladies from the retirement home
arrive exactly at ten to swim.
Slowly they submerge their bodies into the water
and float atop the swimming lanes,
only their eyes sparkling under pink bathing caps.

From time to time they turn over on their backs
and flutter as though drowning in a larger sense
and their limbs, which have merged into each other
until no longer worthy of their names,
pop up here and there out of the ripples
as though someone up there had given up on trifles such as these.

But we true swimmers who tear through the water,
our tan bodies shining in the sun
our muscles celebrating movement,
bursting out of the depths of the water
and diving in again with filled lungs,
find it hard to overcome our secret pleasure
in shooting by like an arrow
and gracefully splashing them
with our youthful mischief.

And we haven't got any pity for these pretenders.
On the contrary:
with broad hints we turn them out
to their rightful place which certainly isn't among us
the swimmers
who don't care to keep abreast just now
of the goal we dive toward.

Poetry Reading

Silence falls over the hall; I hatch in the spotlight.

Dancers' legs inside mine restrain their pirouettes,
the unbelievable soprano in my chest
threatens to burst forth and shatter the large glass windows
but I don't budge.

The poetry fascist raises my hands to orate something overwhelming
about the race of bards
and the entertainer inside me
wants to amuse
until you poke your elbows into each others' ribs
bursting with laughter like comrades-in-comedy
.but I don't budge.

I freeze at the microphone scarecrow
leaning over my pages
and read into the darkness quickly
the words I thought of so slowly.

The Peacock

See how he struts, this splendid swell
who preferred beauty to flight

how he approaches slowly,
with conceit,
his tail swishing and vibrating the eye-fan.
One hundred flamenco dancers
suddenly thrill you from its folds
with purple, mandala eyes.

See how he struts
in all this turquoise,
how he wears his crown,
never turning to gaze
at his own beauty,
he approaches us now,
his tiny head
stuck in the center of the fan like a thumb.

This swell is none other
than a chicken stuffed with whining;
look away and listen to his voice:

neither cat nor owl,
exposing sorrow at the heart of beauty,
the everyday bird under the feathers.

Between the Trees and the Non-Trees

I'm not going anywhere.
I'm too dilapidated to be moved
out of context,
and my laziness tends to stay
where it is,
settling down in a familiar space
at evening,
on the steps,
imagination sated,
my hunting eyes resting
in the sockets of my head.

Why should I get up,
come and go,
stir things up
because of a perfumed orchard
whose breath
I inhale—

Palm fronds wipe away
from the sky's windshield
the words remaining when love has gone
and the ravens too relax one by one
inside the cypress
like blood inside silence.

Thought doesn't covet
its contents.
I just
am here
between the trees and the non-trees,

my door wide open,
the soft night beckoned into the house.

Papua, New Guinea

I love to say Papua, New Guinea.
Otherwise I wouldn't have come here.

My husband Antonio hugs me from behind
before he falls asleep
and whispers:
love me more than I love you.

I stroke his face and love him more
than he loves me.
I don't mind if for a week
I love him more, after all
the Portuguese ambassador has a hard life:
the superpowers threaten
and his sleep is restless, wandering
toward the golden age of colonialism;
words like Angola, Macau, Cochin, and Nampula
sail past like ancient wooden boats in his blood,
turn his snores into a lament and more than once
he chokes, anxious, beaten;
he deserves more love.

I am generous and fill
the new arms holding me
while a strange heart pleads at my back
because the birds in Papua, New Guinea, are colorful
their voices so sweet and seductive behind the curtain
where the moon sheds light on my former life too.

What a talented chameleon I am.
When I crawl over Papua, New Guinea,
I change my colors to its colors,
when I crawl over Antonio's body
I change my colors to his because you have to
take from life everything it gives
and I'm taking.
That is I'm giving.

My husband is extremely neat.
Even the pope hung on our bedroom wall
smiles in satisfaction at such ideal order:
shoes lined up,
shirt and pants folded,
wristwatch on the dresser.

My husband hates my sleeping with a watch.
But at night I love the orchestrated pulse
of heartbeats and the digital tick tock,
and the ironic space stretched between them.

Now I snuggle against his agreeable body,
and the gold Jesus dangling flaccid from his neck
tickles me gently.

I'm Jewish and we are naked.
What does Pope John,
robed and wearing a miter, scepter in hand,
think about us?

One, two, three, four,
I'm the wife of the ambassador.

Caress

All of us here —
the hot-blooded ones who run about over the earth
and those already cold and buried underneath,
hunters of joy and deserters of suffering,
are granted one crystalline moment
by the angels, out of generosity or for amusement's sake,
a caress of light that people feel in their distraction —
and we embrace now, holding tight,
joining love to love

and we look at one another
at the miracle of matchless faces,
and touch one another
with wondrous fingertips whose wisdom is different from our own,
with a broad smile and nonviolent square teeth
bared to each other,
a thrilling, hot and hesitant contact
(because the other is always an image too strong to bear,
a riddle whose solution is only hinted
in a glance like a mirror)

and compassion —
the warm breath blowing over the universe —
mellows our flesh always rushing onward,
drawing out our buried inner cry,
while something watches through the chinks inside,
something up there always
watches,
with pity because we are human,
with compassion for the shoulder blades so longing for flight —

November 4, 1995

Something in the shoulders
weighs down
something   some
thing
in the neck

something *oof*
limps in the heart
de-eep inside
de-eep

something in the room
the things
the nearness of objects
or the light
something in the light

something outside
in the branches
or the ravens
their voices

or something in the world
hard to know
the pain

something
truly expected

sorrow
here

something very
oof

Nocturne

1.

Inside the house
everything is stocked up:
sugar in the jar,
bread in the bread
box,
knife in the drawer,
food in the pot
and evil spirits
in the curtain folds,
all stacked up,
pillowcases
top sheets
underpants
bras
everything in stock—
music in record grooves,
and the rat in the attic
of discarded belongings.

2.

If the woman gets up from her bed
and opens the refrigerator
you might see her face
you might see her glance
in the cheese staring back from its holes,
but in that pale glow,
you see her hunger openmouthed
for a different light,
not the flickering blue
of the television set,
not the red emitted
by the alarm clock,
nor the moon's neon
burnishing the chandelier of her soul.
She needs
a different light
in the night waiting like a black leather chair
to swallow her up.

3.

Not for nothing I stand here in the evening
bent over the sink
manning my station
singing to the distance:
row your boat

because everything that can
leaves the earth:
chimney smoke
prayer
jumps for joy.

But the members of the family breathe
in their sleep, the Lord is their shepherd

and under the house the groundwater
and under the water
the lava of apathy.

Transistor Muezzin

The transistor muezzin rises among the fruit trees—
barefoot Hassan bound to my land
kneads the evening dough from Jewish flour
"too fine, ya Hagi"—that's me.
I've closed my sorting eyes after a day's harvest,
and squat with him over the fire he stokes.

We plan tomorrow's peaches
over a hand-rolled cigarette and the local Europa brand.
"Ya Hagi," his Arabic sigh
leans on the consonants
of my garbled Hungarian name.

In these photosynthesis twilights,
his hands run over a piece of tin
casting a spell with pita.
Hassan builds palaces of legends for me,
Gaza's *Thousand and One Nights*,
his body a supple viper,
his eyes an answer to the fire.

White Chicken

In the middle of
Thursday
I stand like a chicken
on the forks of my legs

if at least
I had
a red
wheelbarrow
glazed with rain
water
I would whiten
beside it
fatefully

but this way
in my situation
I effect
no change
rather I live,
not for my own sake,
with a cockscomb
on my head.

Revelation

Very early one morning
I saw on my clothesline
a pink angel caught by a clothespin
and a black kitten
underneath
trying to catch
its sleeve.

Horse

Can this be the one and only horse
whose skin quivers under my hand?

Can this be the sea neighing
manes of foam,
can this be the soul horse?

Can this be the dream horse,
winged, eating from the palm of my hand,
the Prussian blue horse?

Can this be my obsessional horse?

The soft foal stamping toward me
under the awning of your eyelashes,
can this be the literary horse?

Oh archetypal horse,
cause of all horses,
can this be the final horse?

Notes

"Olive Tree": 7

The last line of the third stanza reads in literal translation from Hebrew: "the uproar of the clearing." "Clearing" signals to the Hebrew reader an Israeli army euphemism for cutting down cultivated olive trees, ostensibly in order to "clear" the sides of the roads from places where terrorists might sit in ambush. The translation of the poem provides an explanation as no equivalent connotation is evoked by the word "clearing" in English.

"Red Hail": 8

The title refers to the code word which would have been used to warn Israeli citizens of missile attacks had Saddam Hussein used them during the second Gulf War in 2003. In the first Gulf War, in 1991, the code word "Viper" was broadcast on Israeli radio and television when such attacks took place.

Biblical references: line 5, Psalms 55:6–7; line 10, Song of Songs 2:14; line 13, Genesis 11:7; line 19, Genesis 8; line 23, Psalms 23:1.

"A Little Prayer for Sunday": 56

Israel has a six-day work week, and Sunday is a regular work day.

"[Someone lit the wax flowers in your garden,]": 29

Agi Mishol's parents, Klara and Joseph Fried, were Holocaust survivors; Klara survived Auschwitz, Joseph a forced labor camp.

"November 4, 1995": 67

The date on which Israeli Prime Minister Yitzhak Rabin was assassinated by a Jewish extremist opposed to peace with the Palestinians. "De-eep inside" is an allusion to the Israeli national anthem, in which the Jewish spirit yearns "de-eep in the heart."

AGI MISHOL was born in 1947 in Hungary and brought to Israel as a very young child. She is the author of twelve books of poetry and the winner of every major Israeli poetry prize, including the first Yehuda Amichai Prize in 2002. Her latest books, *New and Selected Works* and *Moment*, recently moved into their fifth and second printings, respectively; a group of her poems have been dramatized in a play, *The Owl Ladies*, and a jazz CD has been based on *Moment*. A teacher of poetry workshops and lecturer in literature, Mishol holds BA and MA degrees in Hebrew literature from Hebrew University in Jerusalem. She lives on a farm in Gedera, Israel.

LISA KATZ was born in New York and moved to Israel in 1983, receiving a PhD on the poetry of Sylvia Plath from the English Department of the Hebrew University, where she teaches literary translation. She serves as co-editor of the Israeli pages of the *Poetry International Web (PIW)* project for world poetry in translation. A volume of her poetry in Hebrew translation will appear in Israel in 2006; an essay on Plath is forthcoming in *European Contributions to American Studies*. She lives in Jerusalem.

Look There has been typeset in Electra, a typeface designed by William Addison Dwiggins (1880–1956), an American designer and typographer. Book design by Wendy Holdman. Composition by Stanton Publication Services, Inc. Manufactured by Thomson-Shore on acid-free paper.